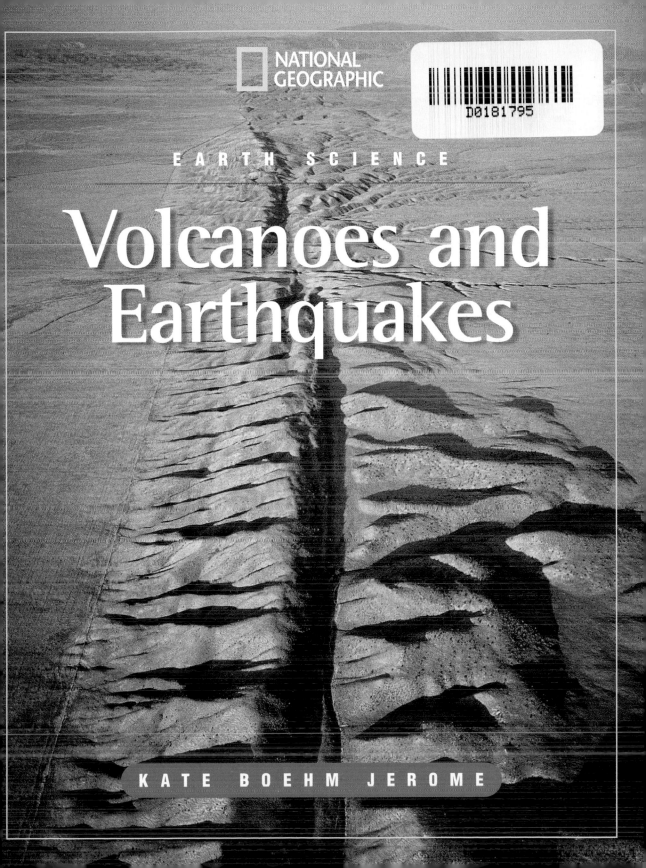

NATIONAL
GEOGRAPHIC

D0181795

EARTH SCIENCE

Volcanoes and Earthquakes

KATE BOEHM JEROME

PICTURE CREDITS
Cover: IFA/Peter Arnold, Inc. Page 1 © James Balog/Stone; pages 2–3 James Richardson; page 4 © Roger Ressmeyer/CORBIS; page 5 David A. Hardy/SPL/Photo Researchers, Inc.; page 6 Pier Paolo Cito/AP; pages 7, 9, 14 Equator Graphics; page 8 Shusei Nagaoka; pages 10, 12, 15, 24 (mid) National Geographic Maps; page 11 Robert S. Patton; pages 13, 24 (low right) © Bourseiller/Hoa-Qui/Photo Researchers, Inc.; page 16 © 1992 Carol Simowitz Photography; page 17 courtesy A.J.'s Sport Stop; pages 18 (top left), 26 art by Stephen R. Wagner; page 18 (low) courtesy Maya Tolstoy; page 19 Chris Butler/SPL/Photo Researchers, Inc.; page 20 Eyal Warshavsky/AP; page 21 Roger Winstead/North Carolina State University Creative Services; page 22 K. and M. Krafft/Photo Researchers, Inc.; page 23 NASA; pages 24–25 (background) © Digital Stock; page 24 (low left) William F. Foshag Collection/Smithsonian Institution Archives; page 25 (low left) © Mark Rykoff Collection/CORBIS; page 25 (low right) © 1995 P.J. Griffiths/Magnum Photos, Inc., page 27 courtesy of the Archives, California Institute of Technology; pages 28–29 Lloyd Wolf.

Back cover: (top to bottom) © Corbis Royalty Free Images, © Fred Bavendam/Minden Pictures, © Robert W. Madden, © Artville, © Layne Kennedy/CORBIS.

Neither the publisher nor the author shall be liable for any damage that may be caused or sustained or result from conducting any of the activities in this book without specifically following instructions, undertaking the activities without proper supervision, or failing to comply with the cautions contained in the book.

Cover photo: Stromboli volcano, Italy

Produced through the worldwide resources of the National Geographic Society, John M. Fahey, Jr., President and Chief Executive Officer; Gilbert M. Grosvenor, Chairman of the Board; Nina D. Hoffman, Executive Vice President and President, Books and School Publishing.

PREPARED BY NATIONAL GEOGRAPHIC SCHOOL PUBLISHING
Ericka Markman, Senior Vice President; Steve Mico, Editorial Director; Barbara Seeber, Editorial Manager; Lynda McMurray, Amy Sarver, Project Editors; Roger B. Hirschland, Consulting Editor; Jim Hiscott, Design Manager; Karen Thompson, Art Director; Kristin Hanneman, Illustrations Manager; Diana Bourdrez, Tom DiGiovanni, Ruth Goldberg, Stephanie Henke, Diana Leskovac, Anne Whittle, Photo Editors; Christine Higgins, Photo Coordinator; Matt Wascavage, Manager of Publishing Services; Sean Philpotts, Production Coordinator.

Production: Clifton M. Brown III, Manufacturing and Quality Control.

CONSULTANT/REVIEWER
Dr. Timothy Cooney, Professor of Earth Science and Science Education, University of Northern Iowa

PROGRAM DEVELOPMENT
Kate Boehm Jerome

BOOK DESIGN
3r1 Group

Published by the National Geographic Society
1145 17th Street, N.W.
Washington, D.C. 20036-4688

ISBN: 0-7922-8874-2

Second Printing January 2003
Printed in Canada.

In 1973 a volcano named Eldfell hurled lava above a town in Iceland.

Contents

A Volcano Awakens

There was panic in the streets. It was an August afternoon in Pompeii, Italy, in A.D. 79. Bits of burning rock and flaming cinders rained down on frightened citizens as they rushed for shelter. There was no place to hide. Mount Vesuvius—the volcano that was supposed to sleep forever—was erupting in fury.

Mount Vesuvius

The next morning, the wealthy Roman trading town of Pompeii was buried. A cloud of ash and poisonous gases had poured down the mountain, killing everyone. The beautiful houses were covered with rubble. The busy city was gone, destroyed by forces from within Earth.

The town of Pompeii was preserved at a moment in time because the ash cloud covered everything at once. Pompeii remained buried for hundreds of years until it was rediscovered in the 1700s. Today scientists still uncover treasures that give us information about the people of Pompeii and what they were doing on the last day of their lives.

Before A.D. 79 there were warning signs that Mount Vesuvius was going to blow. Earthquakes had shaken the area around the mountain for at least 15 years. Yet no one connected the earthquakes with the growing danger inside the volcano.

This is a book about the forces inside Earth that sometimes change its exterior. Some changes take place slowly over time. Other changes happen quickly through the violent shaking of an **earthquake** or the explosive eruption of a **volcano**. How do these changes happen? Read on to find out how our planet rocks and rolls.

A plaster cast preserves the final moments of a resident of Pompeii.

The Earth Erupts

It's been almost 2,000 years since Vesuvius buried Pompeii. Now another volcano rumbles and shakes in Italy. Mount Etna, the most active volcano in Europe, towers more than 3,310 meters (10,860 feet) above the island of Sicily. More than 200 explosions have been recorded since 1500 B.C.

Mount Etna erupted violently during the summer of 2001. Smoke and ash shot thousands of meters into the air. Melted rock reaching the surface of Earth, called **lava,** spilled from the volcano and crept down the mountain. Airplanes dumped thousands of liters of water on the lava to try to cool it, so it would harden and stop moving toward the cities below the volcano. People living in the area carried umbrellas to protect themselves from the constant rain of ash and debris. The airport nearby temporarily closed because the thick layer of ash on the runway made it unsafe for planes to take off or land. For weeks people in Sicily watched and waited as scientists swarmed over the mountain to gather data.

Finally, Etna quieted down again before it caused too much damage. Although some property was lost, few people were forced to leave. The people who live around Mount Etna felt lucky—knowing the outcome could have been much worse. They are used to the benefits and threats of an active volcano. In this agricultural region they depend on the rich soil that eventually comes from the lava. Yet they know that the next eruption could drive them from their homes.

Volcanoes are a hazard that humans live with but cannot control. How and why do volcanoes erupt? The answer lies not only inside Earth but also at its surface.

Lava and smoke spew from Mount Etna on July 25, 2001.

Layers Within Earth

Volcanoes form because of the action of **magma**, or hot, melted rock. Where does this magma come from? Let's look at the layers of Earth to find out.

The ground that you stand on is the outermost layer of the planet. Called the **crust**, this top layer includes not only the land you can see but also the land on the ocean floor. The crust is not the same thickness everywhere on the planet.

Earth's Layers

Crust

Mantle

Outer core

Inner core

The crust of the continents is usually about 32 kilometers (20 miles) thick. The ocean crust is, on average, only 5 to 8 kilometers (3 to 5 miles) thick.

Even at its thickest point, the crust is still very thin compared with the next layer of Earth, called the **mantle**. This middle layer of Earth is about 2,900 kilometers (1,800 miles) thick. This layer is where magma forms.

The thickest layer of Earth, called the **core**, is right below the mantle. The outer core is so hot that scientists believe it is a liquid layer of melted iron and nickel. This layer is about 2,250 kilometers (1,400 miles) thick. The inner core is about 1,300 kilometers (800 miles) thick and is even hotter. The temperature can reach 6000°C (10,832°F). Can you imagine how hot the inner core of Earth must be if it's 100 times hotter than our worst summer day?

Movement at the Surface

How does magma get to the surface of Earth to form volcanoes? The answer may surprise you.

The ground beneath your feet feels firm. It might seem there's no way that this solid layer of Earth can be moving. But guess what! It's moving slowly all the time.

How do we know this? We can trace the evidence all the way back to the 1500s when explorers first mapped the continents. People noticed then that the coastlines of some continents seemed to fit together like pieces of a jigsaw puzzle. This puzzle fit was one of the pieces of evidence that led to a new conclusion about movement on Earth's surface. In 1912 a German scientist named Alfred Wegener proposed that millions of years ago there was only one huge land mass, or supercontinent. He named the supercontinent Pangaea. Wegener thought that about 200 million years ago, Pangaea split into continents that eventually drifted apart into the land masses we know today. Wegener's idea that continents can move became known as **continental drift**.

Continental Drift

PANGAEA

200 million years ago

135 million years ago

65 million years ago

Today

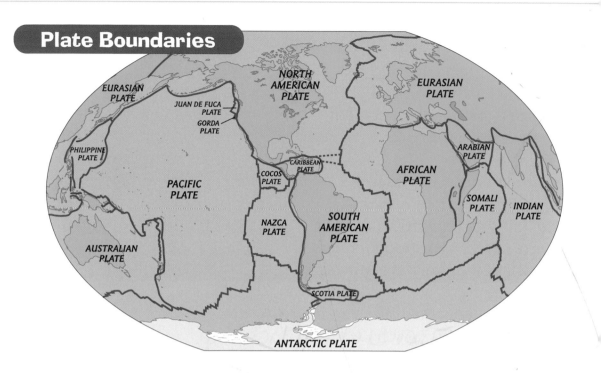

Plate Boundaries

In the 1960s scientists began to realize that seafloors, as well as continents, could move. A series of underwater mountains, called mid-ocean ridges, was discovered. New crust forms at these ridges when magma pushes up through cracks in the ridges. As magma cools, it hardens into solid rock. This new rock pushes the older rock material to each side of the ridge causing the seafloor to spread apart.

Plate Tectonics Explains It

Scientists now had evidence that both the continents and the ocean floor could move. Now they needed to explain how this movement could happen. In the 1960s the theory of **plate tectonics** did just that.

The theory of plate tectonics says that Earth's crust, along with the solid upper part of Earth's mantle, is broken into about 20 huge slabs of rock called **plates**. Magma rises up between the edges of some plates, forcing the plates apart. The plates can move because they slide over the hotter, softer rocks in the mantle beneath them.

Does this mean the continents we live on are actually moving all the time? Yes. Each continent on Earth is part of one or more plates and moves with those plates. The movement of plates is very slow—only a few centimeters a year—so we don't notice the motion. But over millions of years, the action of the moving plates reshapes continents and ocean floors.

Plates move away from each other, slide past each other, and even run into each other. When this happens, there is action on Earth's surface.

Where the Action Is

Is there a connection between moving plates and volcanoes? Well, it seems that one often leads to the other. That is, volcanoes may form where plates move apart, where plates meet, and even in the center of plates. Plate movement takes place very slowly and over millions of years.

Umbrellas protect people as ash from Pinatubo's 1991 eruption in the Philippines covers a nearby village.

Ring of Fire

Plates Moving Apart

As plates move away from each other, cracks in Earth's crust can form. When magma rises through these cracks, volcanoes form along the edges of the plates. These volcanoes are called **rift volcanoes**, and they usually form at the bottom of the ocean along mid-ocean ridges. Sometimes the new crust of a rift volcano builds up over so many years that it eventually rises above the water. A rift volcano near Iceland rose above the Atlantic Ocean in 1963. This volcano became the island of Surtsey.

More than 80 percent of the active volcanoes in the world are found around the plates that form the floor of the Pacific Ocean. This ring of volcanoes is known as the Pacific Ring of Fire.

Plates Crashing Together

When two plates collide, or come together, several things can happen. If there is a continent on both sides of the plates, the crust of the continents can bend and wrinkle. (Think about the bending and wrinkling of metal when two cars collide.) This wrinkling can eventually form mountains. The Himalaya mountain range in India and Nepal was formed

Visitors compare Washington State's Mount St. Helens to a photograph taken before its 1980 eruption.

this way. This range includes the highest mountains in the world.

If there is a continent on one plate and an ocean floor on the other plate when the plates collide, a volcano can form. This is because the ocean plate slides under the continental plate. As the plate slides deep into the mantle, the rock melts to form magma. Pressure then forces the magma through weak spots in the crust. In time, the magma can break through a hole, or **vent**, in Earth's crust. At the surface, the magma is called lava, which cools and hardens into rock. With many eruptions, the lava, along with cinders and ash, piles up and up until the volcano becomes a mountain.

Activity Underneath the Plates

Not all volcanoes form at the edges of plates. Sometimes they pop up in the middle of a plate. How can this happen?

Scientists think that in some places magma rises to the crust from deep within the mantle. These places are called **hot spots**. As a plate moves over a hot spot, magma can melt through the plate and form a volcano. (Remember that Earth's crust is not very thick under the oceans.) If the volcano erupts many times, it can build up to form an island. Eventually, the plate moves. Since the island has become part of the plate, it moves with the plate. However, the hot spot under the plate stays in the same place. A second volcano can now form over the hot spot. If this volcano erupts many times, another island can form. Over time as the plate continues to move, it can take that island with it too. Then another volcano can form and grow into another island on the same hot spot. The chain of Hawaiian Islands formed this way over millions of years.

How Island Chains Form From Hot Spots

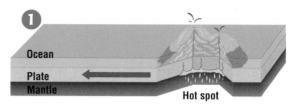

Magma from the hot spot rises through the plate. (The plate consists of the crust and solid, upper part of the mantle.) An island is formed after many eruptions.

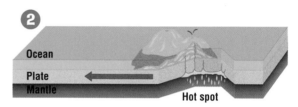

As the plate moves, the volcano moves with it. The hot spot remains in the same place.

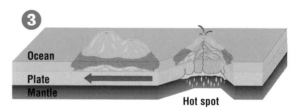

The first volcano stops erupting. A second volcano forms at the hot spot. After numerous eruptions, another island is formed.

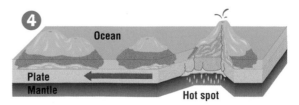

The plate continues to move. The two islands travel away from the hot spot. The process repeats as another new volcano forms over the hot spot.

Thinking Like a Scientist: Predicting

Sometimes it is helpful for scientists to make a **prediction**; that is, they form an idea about what will happen in the future. A prediction is more likely to be correct if it is based on information that comes from observing what has happened in similar situations.

The chain of Hawaiian Islands was formed over millions of years as the plate on which the islands now sit moved slowly over a hot spot. Look at the drawing below and see if you can make some predictions based on what you know about hot spots.

- Which island in the chain do you think is the oldest? Why?

- What do you think will happen if Loihi continues to erupt and grow?

Hawaii's Chain of Islands

A Niihau
B Kauai
C Oahu
D Molokai
E Maui
F Hawaii
G Lanai
H Kahoolawe

15

Chapter 2

The Earth Quakes

It was World Series night, October 17, 1989. Thousands of baseball fans packed Candlestick Park in San Francisco, California. The first ball was about to be thrown. Suddenly it wasn't just the baseball getting pitched. The fans and the stadium were all shaking. An earthquake was rocking the park!

Candlestick Park

About 60 people were killed in the earthquake of 1989, and many highways were destroyed. What causes an earthquake like this?

When the Crust Cracks

Most earthquakes take place along the boundaries between two plates. When plates move, great force is placed on the rocky slabs that make up the plate. If too much pressure is placed on it, the rock will eventually break. Then a **fault** is formed. Faults are cracks in Earth's crust. When rocks along a fault move, the ground shakes. That's an earthquake.

Most faults are deep within Earth's crust, and you can't see them. However, some faults occur at the surface. The San Andreas Fault is a huge crack in Earth's surface that runs for almost 1,200 kilometers (750 miles) near the coast of California. This fault forms the boundary along which the Pacific plate slides past the North American plate. The earthquake that shook the World Series game in Candlestick Park occurred along the San Andreas Fault.

1989 World Series souvenirs

Another big earthquake occurred in San Francisco in 1906 when a section of rock slipped along the San Andreas Fault. San Francisco suffered great damage not only from the quake but also from the fires that broke out from overturned stoves, broken gas pipes, and damaged electrical wiring. The fires raged through the city for three days.

Why do you think certain areas are struck by earthquakes over and over again?

Earthquake Diagram

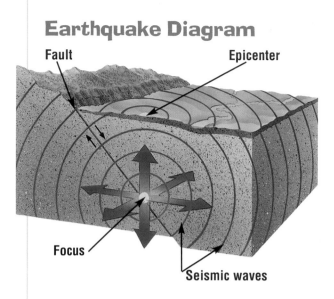

Fault

Epicenter

Focus

Seismic waves

Seismic Waves

The point where an earthquake starts is called its **focus**. This spot is usually somewhere underground. When rocks begin to slide at the focus, vibrations travel out in waves. Have you ever tossed a pebble into a pond? If so, you might have noticed that waves ripple out in all directions from the point where the stone hit the water. The same thing happens in an earthquake. Vibrations, called **seismic waves**, travel out from the quake's focus in all directions. The point where the waves first reach Earth's surface is called the **epicenter**. The epicenter is right above the focus; most of the damage from the earthquake usually occurs at the epicenter.

Scientists use an instrument called a **seismograph** to measure seismic waves. In steady conditions the pen of a seismograph will draw a straight line on recording paper. If the Earth starts to shake, the paper on the seismograph will move up and down. Scientists study the lines that are recorded to determine the epicenter and the strength of an earthquake.

Why do you think waves from the same earthquake can cause more damage in one area than another?

Focus On ▶▶▶

Maya Tolstoy: Marine Seismologist

Maya Tolstoy studies earthquakes that often don't make the news. She is a marine seismologist, which means she watches for earthquakes that happen on the ocean floor. Maya uses underwater microphones to listen for earthquakes. She hopes to learn more about the mid-ocean ridges by studying the earthquakes and volcanoes that form them.

The Damage Is Done

What kinds of damage can an earthquake cause? That depends on its location and **magnitude**, or the amount of energy it releases. An earthquake's magnitude is measured by the strength of the waves recorded on the seismograph.

The most immediate effect of an earthquake is shaking ground. Sometimes the shaking lasts only a few seconds; other times it can go on for several minutes. Often the shaking makes buildings crack and collapse. Earthquake vibrations also can loosen sandy soil and mix it with nearby water causing the land to slip and sink, along with homes and other structures on it. Sometimes earthquakes rip roads and other surfaces apart. Entire buildings can suddenly fall into these openings.

Earthquakes that occur underwater can trigger a **tsunami**, which is an enormous ocean wave. In the open ocean, tsunamis are barely noticeable. As tsunamis move to shallower water near land and hit the floor of the ocean, the waves get larger. The waves may rise as high as a ten-story building. When the waves break on land, they can cause great destruction.

Illustration of a tsunami approaching a harbor

Chapter 3

Life on the Edge

An earthquake shakes the city. Buildings fall. People might be trapped deep inside the rubble of concrete and debris.

Earthquake survivors view the damage from an earthquake in Turkey in 1999.

Rescue workers launch a robotic inchworm into the pipes of the building to try to find signs of life. The tiny robot creeps deep into a collapsed building through the pipe system. This robotic snake has a tiny video camera and lights. The little robot can go through tight twists and turns. It also can carry sensors to detect movement. If a trapped person is tapping on an object for help, the tiny robot detects the vibrations and sends information back to rescue workers. This helps the workers zero in on the area where the person is trapped. Valuable time is saved.

Although this rescue method is not yet a reality, inventors from the College of Engineering at North Carolina State University hope that someday it will be. After an earthquake, one of the biggest problems is finding survivors in time. The researchers at North Carolina State know that pipes often are unbroken when a building collapses. So they designed a robot that can crawl through the pipes to find survivors.

Although we can't stop volcanoes and earthquakes from happening, technology can help us predict and prepare for these natural events. The more information we can gather, the better we can protect ourselves from disasters when they do occur.

Pipe-crawling robot

Predicting Volcanoes and Earthquakes

Unfortunately, many dangerous volcanic eruptions and earthquakes occur without warning. However, scientists are making progress figuring out how to predict them.

The seismograph that measures earthquakes also is a useful tool for predicting volcanic eruptions. Remember that the city of Pompeii experienced earthquakes for 15 years before Mount Vesuvius exploded. These earthquakes were warning signs. When magma begins to rise, it often causes quakes. In March 1980 the increased activity of seismographs helped alert scientists that magma was on the move in Mount St. Helens in Washington State. Because of warnings from these and other instruments, most people left the area before this volcano erupted.

Many other instruments help scientists detect movement within Earth. A tiltmeter detects changes in the tilt of the land. Lasers also are used to make sensitive measurements. Scientists even use satellites to measure the movement of the crust over hundreds of kilometers. Any movement can signal that an earthquake or an eruption may be coming.

Researchers wear fire-resistant suits when studying volcanoes up close.

Dante II

laser equipment. These systems allow Dante to build a 3-D computer image of the volcano. Dante also can analyze high-temperature gases that help scientists predict when an eruption might occur.

Recognizing patterns and understanding how volcanoes and earthquakes occur offers some protection from these powerful forces. Respecting the forces of nature while minimizing the danger to humans is a constant challenge.

Exploring to the Limit

One way to learn more about a volcano is to crawl down inside it. However, scientists often have to wear protective clothing just to get close to an active crater. Poisonous gases, hot steam, and flying rocks make the task very dangerous and sometimes impossible.

In 1994 scientists built a robot, called Dante II, to help them explore volcanoes. Dante II looks like a big spider with eight long legs and several antennas. Dante II is equipped with video cameras and

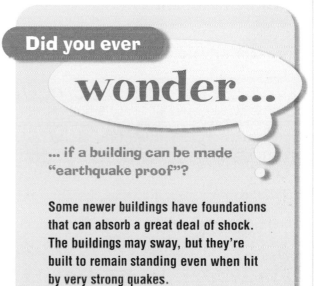

Did you ever

wonder...

... if a building can be made "earthquake proof"?

Some newer buildings have foundations that can absorb a great deal of shock. The buildings may sway, but they're built to remain standing even when hit by very strong quakes.

Earthquakes and Volcanic Eruptions of the 20th Century

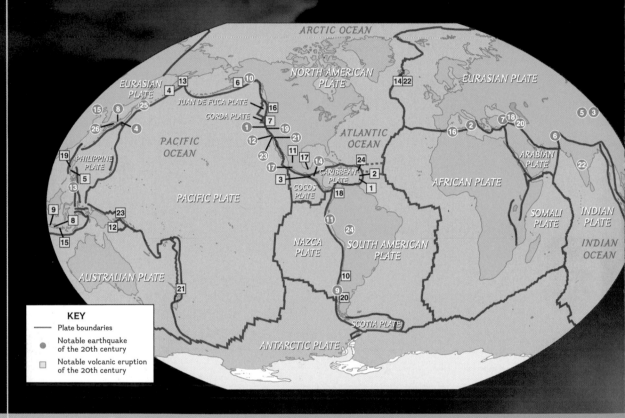

ARCTIC OCEAN

NORTH AMERICAN PLATE

EURASIAN PLATE

EURASIAN PLATE

JUAN DE FUCA PLATE

GORDA PLATE

PACIFIC OCEAN

ATLANTIC OCEAN

ARABIAN PLATE

PHILIPPINE PLATE

PACIFIC PLATE

CARIBBEAN PLATE

COCOS PLATE

AFRICAN PLATE

SOMALI PLATE

INDIAN PLATE

INDIAN OCEAN

NAZCA PLATE

SOUTH AMERICAN PLATE

AUSTRALIAN PLATE

SCOTIA PLATE

ANTARCTIC PLATE

KEY
— Plate boundaries
● Notable earthquake of the 20th century
□ Notable volcanic eruption of the 20th century

Paricutín, Mexico • 1943

Pinatubo, Philippines • 1991

Earthquake magnitudes are based on the moment-magnitude scale that scientists use as a more precise measurement than the commonly known Richter scale.

Notable Earthquakes

1	1906	San Francisco, California, USA (7.7)
2	1908	Messina, Italy (7.0)
3	1920	Gansu and Shaanxi, China (8.3)
4	1923	Tokyo, Japan (7.9)
5	1927	Qinghai, China (7.7)
6	1935	Quetta, Pakistan (8.1)
7	1939	Erzincan, Turkey (7.6)
8	1948	Fukui, Japan (6.9)
9	1960	Southern Chile (9.5)
10	1964	Southern Alaska, USA (9.2)
11	1970	Northern Peru (7.9)
12	1971	San Fernando, California, USA (6.7)
13	1976	Mindanao, Philippines (8.1)
14	1976	Guatemala (7.6)
15	1976	Tangshan, China (7.4)
16	1980	El Asnam, Algeria (7.1)
17	1985	Michoacán, Mexico (8.1)
18	1988	Armenia (6.8)
19	1989	Loma Prieta, California, USA (7.0)
20	1990	Western Iran (7.5)
21	1992	Landers, California, USA (7.3)
22	1993	Latur, India (6.2)
23	1994	Northridge, California, USA (6.7)
24	1994	Northern Bolivia (8.3)
25	1994	Kuril Islands, Japan (8.3)
26	1995	Kobe, Japan (6.9)

Notable Volcanic Eruptions

1	1902	Soufrière, St. Vincent
2	1902	Mount Peléc, Martinique
3	1902	Santa María, Guatemala
4	1907	Ksudach, Kamchatka, Russia
5	1911	Taal, Luzon, Philippines
6	1912	Katmai/Novarupta, Alaska, USA
7	1914	Lassen Peak, California, USA
8	1919	Kelut, Java, Indonesia
9	1930	Merapi, Java, Indonesia
10	1932	Quizapú, Chile
11	1943	Paricutín, Mexico
12	1951	Lamington, Papua New Guinea
13	1956	Bezymyannaya, Kamchatka, Russia
14	1963	Surtsey, Iceland
15	1963	Agung, Bali, Indonesia
16	1980	Mount St. Helens, Washington, USA
17	1982	El Chichón, Mexico
18	1985	Nevado del Ruiz, Colombia
19	1991	Pinatubo, Luzon, Philippines
20	1991	Cerro Hudson, Chile
21	1995	Ruapehu, New Zealand
22	1996	Grímsvötn, Iceland
23	1997	Rabaul Caldera, Papua New Guinea
24	1997	Soufriere Hills, Montserrat

San Francisco, California • 1906   Kobe, Japan • 1995

Street cracked by the earthquake April 18, 1906. San Francisco, California.

Predicting

Being able to predict, or form an idea about what is going to happen, is an important skill. In fact, it can save your life. For example, you can predict what might happen if you try crossing a busy street against the light. So you wait for the WALK sign and check carefully for cars before crossing.

Scientists still cannot predict the exact time a major earthquake will occur. However, they can make fairly accurate predictions of what the damage might be if earthquakes of a certain magnitude occur in certain areas. They make these predictions based on knowledge of the damage that earthquakes have caused in the past. Predicting what an earthquake's effect might be on a city can help officials prepare for emergency situations. Predictions also can help architects and engineers design safer buildings and bridges. The diagram below illustrates an earthquake and shows three cities that might be affected by it.

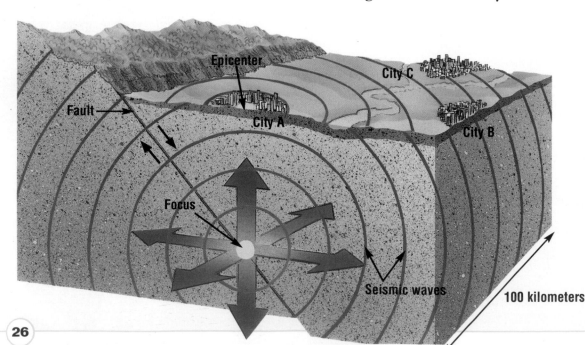

Epicenter

City C

Fault

City A

City B

Focus

Seismic waves

100 kilometers

Practice the Skill

Answer the following questions to predict how the earthquake might affect the three cities. Assume all three cities have similar buildings and are built on similar ground. You may need to refer to the Richter scale at right.

1. Which city would be affected most by the earthquake?

2. Suppose the earthquake measured 3.8 on the Richter scale. What kind of damage would you predict for City C?

3. Suppose the earthquake measured 6.5 on the Richter scale. What kind of damage would you predict for City A? For City B? For City C?

Focus On >>>

Charles Richter: Seismologist

In 1935 Charles Richter came up with a scale that compared the energy of earthquakes. Using his scale, how much damage would you expect from an earthquake with a magnitude of 7.0?

Richter Scale:

Rating	Effect Near Epicenter
Less than 3.5	Not usually felt
3.5–5.4	Felt by many people; minor damage
5.5–6.0	Some damage
6.1–6.9	Much damage
7.0–7.9	Severe damage
8 or greater	Total destruction

Check It Out

Suppose much of City B is built on landfill, clay, and sandy soil, while the other cities are built on solid rock. How would that affect the kind of damage you predict for City B after the 6.5 earthquake?

How Magma Moves

As you know, magma comes from deep within Earth. You can make a model of the way it moves.

Materials
- ✔ Plastic glass
- ✔ Water
- ✔ Red food coloring
- ✔ Sponge
- ✔ Paper towel
- ✔ Medicine dropper
- ✔ Vegetable oil
- ✔ Hand lens

SAFETY TIP: When working with water, wipe up any spills immediately.

Explore

1 Fill the plastic glass 3/4 full with water. Mix two drops of food coloring into the water.

2 Put the sponge on the paper towel. Place two dropperfuls of vegetable oil onto the center of the sponge. *(See photograph A.)*

A

3 Then fold the sponge, so the oil is on the outside of the sponge. Turn the sponge on its side and place it in the glass. *(See photograph B.)* Make sure the entire sponge is slightly below the surface of the water.

4 Use a hand lens to look through the glass at the oil and the sponge.

5 Record what you see happening.

B

Think

What happens to the oil when the sponge is placed in the water? How is this action like the action of magma in Earth? How is this model different from the action of magma in Earth?

Science Notebook

FACTS AND FIGURES

- Mauna Loa in Hawaii is the world's largest volcano. It rises more than 9,150 meters (30,000 feet) above the ocean floor.

- One of the deadliest earthquakes in recent history occurred in the Chinese city of Tangshan in July 1976. More than half a million people lost their lives.

- In 1933 a tsunami hit the coast of Japan with a wave height of more than 14 meters (45 feet). It killed almost 3,000 people.

- In 1991 scientists predicted that Mount Pinatubo in the Philippines would soon erupt. Seventy-five thousand people were evacuated before it erupted June 15, 1991. Even though 300 people died, quick action by authorities saved thousands of lives.

BOOKS TO READ

Knight, Lindsay. *Volcanoes and Earthquakes*. Time Life Books, 1995.

Haduch, Bill. *Earthquake!* Dutton Books, 1999.

WEBSITES TO VISIT

Learn about the basics of earthquakes:
whyfiles.org/094quake/index.html

Learn about volcanoes at this website supported by NASA:
volcano.und.nodak.edu

Glossary

continental drift – theory proposed by Alfred Wegener in 1912 that says the continents once all fit together but then split and drifted apart

core – the deepest layer of Earth

crust – outermost layer of Earth

earthquake – a shaking or trembling of Earth

epicenter – the point on the surface of Earth where an earthquake is first felt. The epicenter is right above the focus.

fault – a crack in Earth's crust where earthquakes occur

focus – the point where an earthquake starts

hot spot – an intensely hot region where magma can burn through a plate and form a volcano

lava – magma that erupts from a volcano and flows onto Earth's surface

magma – hot, melted rock beneath the surface of Earth

magnitude – the amount of energy an earthquake releases

mantle – the layer of Earth between the crust and core

plate – one of many huge slabs of rock that make up Earth's outer shell

plate tectonics – the theory that Earth's crust and solid upper part of the mantle are made up of about 20 huge plates that are always moving very slowly

prediction – an idea of what will happen in the future

rift volcano – volcano that forms along the gaps at the edges of plates that are moving apart

seismic wave – wave that travels out from an earthquake

seismograph *(SIZE-muh-graf)* – an instrument that measures seismic waves

tsunami *(tsu-NAH-mee)* – a giant wave caused by an underwater disturbance

vent – the main opening in the top of a volcano through which magma and hot gases escape

volcano – opening in the surface of Earth through which hot, melted rock and gases rise

Index